ELBOW ROOM

ELBOW ROOM

OLIVER ST. JOHN GOGARTY

DUELL, SLOAN AND PEARCE
NEW YORK

To Major Eugene Kinkead

Grateful acknowledgment is made to editors of THE NEW YORKER *and* THE NEW YORK TIMES *for permission to reprint poems appearing in this book.*

CONTENTS

ELBOW ROOM

THE FORGE

The forge is dark
The better to show
The birth of the spark
And the Iron's glow.
The forge is dark
That the smith may know
When to strike the blow
On the luminous arc
As he shapes the shoe.

The bellows blows on the dampened slack,
The coal now glows in the heart of the black.
The smith no longer his arm need raise
To the chain of the bellows that makes the blaze.
I see him search where the blue.flames are
In the heart of the fire to find the bar,
With winking grooves from elbow to wrist
As he tightens the tongs in his bawdy fist,
As he hands the bar to his fidgety son
Who holds it well on the anvil down
Till he raises the hammer that stands on its head
And brings it down with a sound like lead,
For fire has muffled the iron's clamour,
While his son beats time with a smaller hammer,

[3]

And the anvil rings like a pair of bells
In time to the beat that the spark expels,
And I am delighted such sounds are made,
For these are the technical sounds of a trade
Whose glad notes rang in the heavens above
Where a blacksmith slept with the Queen of Love.
The horse is looking without reproof
For the leathery lap that has hugged his hoof:
The patient horse that has cast a shoe;
The horse is looking; and I look too
Through the open door to the cindered pool
That a streamlet leaves for the wheels to cool.
I meditate in the forge light dim
On the will of God in the moving limb,
And I realise that the lift and fall
Of the sledge depends on the Mover of All.

O lend me your sledge for a minute or two,
O smith, I have something profound to do!
I swing it up in the half-lit dark,
And down it comes in a straightening arc
On the anvil now where there's nothing to glow.
What matter? No matter! A blow is a blow!
I swing it up in my bulging fists
To prove that the outside world exists;
That the world exists and is more than naught—
As the pale folk hold—but a form of thought.
You think me mad? but it does me good,
A blow is a measure of hardihood.
I lift the sledge, and I strike again
Bang! for the world inside the brain;

And if there's another of which you have heard
Give me the sledge and I'll strike for a third.

I have frightened the horse, though I meant it not:
(Which proves that he is not a form of my thought).
I shall frighten myself if I ramble on
With philosophy where there is room for none.
I was going to say that the blacksmith's blow—
If I were the Master of Those who Know—
Would give me a thesis to demonstrate
That Man may fashion but not create.
He melts the mountains. He turns their lode
Against themselves like a Titan god.
He challenges Time by recording thought,
Time stands; but yet he makes nothing from naught,
He bends Form back to the shapes it wore
Before the dawn of the days of yore;
He bends Form back to the primal state;
He changes all, but he cannot create;
And tamper he cannot with the ways of Fate.
Between ourselves it is just as well,
If Man ruled Fate he would make Life hell.

What have I done?
What shall I do?
                    No wonder Pegasus cast a shoe
When I succumbed to the English curse
Of mixing philosophy up with verse.
I can imagine a poet teaching;
But who can imagine a poet preaching?
Soon I shall hear the blacksmith's scoff:

"The ground is sticky, they can't take off!"
When I press with my thighs and begin to urge
The heavenly horse from the earthly forge.

I know right well that a song should be
Airy and light as the leaf of a tree,
Light as a leaf that lies on the wind,
Or a bird that sings as he sits on the linde,
And shakes the spray when he dives for flight
With bright drops sprinkling the morning light;
For song that is lovely is light and aloof,
As the sparks that fly up from the well-shod hoof.

THE BLACKBIRD IN THE TOWN

The music Finn loved was that which brought joy to the heart and light to the countenance, the music of the blackbird of Letter Lee.

Here behind the huddled houses
Which the squalid gardens break
Golden bill my heart arouses
With his golden gurgling beak;
Disregarding all the squalor
In a backyard after rain
Boldly lifts the Bird of Valour
His mellifluous refrain:
Lifts the fanfare heroes hearkened
When his singing shook the dew
In the dells by oak-leaves darkened
Eighteen hundred years ago,
Sings the song to which Finn listened
When he first was famed and named,
And the ruffian blue eyes glistened
For Finn loved the bird untamed.
I too hear the self-same whistle
Purling all around his nest
Singing to the eggs that nestle
Underneath a browner breast,
Hear the wordless notes transcendant

Over every human rhyme,
Careless, sweet and independent
Of all circumstance of Time;
And I think: though many wrongs ache
In my heart, what matters wrong,
If I sing but for the Song's sake,
If I reach as brave a song,
Filled with fight and self-reliance
Warring with all evil chance,
Loudly whistling my defiance
In the slums of circumstance,
Or, above all, go one better
And, ignoring human wrong,
Bravely as the Bird of Letter
Fling on air a heartless song.

ELBOW ROOM

Astronomers describe a place,
Seen through a crack in the vault of Space
So dark, so absolute, so far,
No light wave from the oldest star
Nor even the thought of God can reach
And fainting fall on that far beach:
Abhorrent and inhuman this
Chineses call, "The Great Abyss."
But I am cheered, for now I know
There's somewhere left for a man to go—
(Always supposing one would care
When dead for going anywhere)
But what a place to make your goal
And lift your head and rouse your soul!
Oh! what a place to speak your mind
Without disquieting mankind!
There's where I would find elbow room
Alone, beyond the crack of doom.

ALL THE PICTURES

I told him he would soon be dead.
"I have seen all the pictures," said
My patient. "And I do not care."
What could a doctor do but stare
In admiration half amused
Because the fearless fellow used
"The pictures" as a metaphor,
And was the first to use it for
Life which he could no longer feel
But only see it as a reel?
Was he not right to be resigned
To the sad wisdom of his mind?
Who wants to live when Life's a sight
Shut from the inner senses quite;
When listless heart and cynic mind
Are closed within a callous rind;
When April with its secret green
Is felt no more but only seen;
And Summer with its dusky meadows
Is no more than a play of shadows;
And Autumn's garish oriflamme
Fades like a flickering skiagram;

And all one's friends are gone, or seem
Shadows of dream beyond a dream?
And woman's love not any mo,
Oh, surely then 'tis time to go
And join the shades that make the Show!

TO LYDIA

What spirit was hoaxed
By your lily-white mesh
From its starry lagoon
On the edge of a cloud
Or the crook of the moon?
What lovely and airy
Capricious and proud
Princess out of faery
Was coaxed and endowed
By the sheath of your flesh
As the moon by a cloud?

As a wing thrills the hand
So your body is thrilled
By this thing from the air
That is held in your glance
And would leap out from there
But that your sweet presence,
So lithe and intense,
Restrains the wild essence
That longs to fly hence
And is but half spilled
To its stars by your glance.

THINKING LONG

When children call you, Grandmamma;
And you with thin dark-veined hands
In silence stroke the heads that, Ah!
Recall the glorious smouldering bands
Of sullen gold that bound your brow,
And him who told you how the light
Burst through them when you combed them low
With sidelong head at fall of night:
Before that vision fades away
Just take this message from the Past:
" 'Tis love that counteracts decay
And lights and makes all Beauty last."
And wonder if the love you spared
To starve the light-heart man of rhyme
Has left him low and you grey-haired,
Though you are old, before your time.

FOG HORNS

The fog horns sound
With a note so prolonged
That the whole air is thronged,
And the sound is to me,
In spite of its crying,
The most satisfying,
The bravest of all the brave sounds of the sea.

From the fjords of the North
The fogs belly forth
Like sails of the long ships
That trouble the earth.
They stand with loose sail
In the fords of the Gael:
From Dark Pool to White Ford the surf-light is pale.

The chronicles say
That the Danes in their day
Took a very great prey
Of women from Howth.
They seem to imply
That the women were shy,
That the women were loath

To be taken from Howth.
From bushy and thrushy, sequestering Howth.
No mists of the Druid
Could halt or undo it
When long ships besetted
The warm sands wave-netted.
In vain might men pray
To be spared the invader
To that kind eye of grey,
To the Saint who regretted
Sea-purple Ben Edar.
They sailed to the town
That is sprung from the sea
Where the Liffey comes down
Down to roll on the Lea.

The fog horns sound
With the very same roar
That was sounded of yore
When they sounded for war.
As the war horns sounded
When men leapt ashore,
And raised up the stane
Where the long ships had grounded.
You hear them again
As they called to the Dane,
And the glens were astounded.
War horns sounded,
And strong men abounded
When Dublin was founded.

Whenever a woman of Moore Street complains,
With hawser of hair
Where the golds and browns are,
And under her arm
A sieve or a dish
Full of flowers or of fish,
I think of that ancient forgotten alarm:
Of horror and grief
As she snatched at the leaf
In tunnels sea-ended that fall to the reef.

It was all Long Ago,
Only now to the slow
Groping in of the ships
In the sunlight's eclipse,
Are the fog horns sounded;
When war horns sounded
War ships could be grounded,
And dynasties founded.
But now they crawl in
With a far louder din
Than the old horns' could be;
And that's as it should be,
Because we put now
In the place of the prow
Of the dragon-head boats
A bow-sprit of notes
With their loud, Safety First!
Where blue-eyed men burst,
And founded a city and founded a thirst!

And founded far more than today could be found:
The lesser the courage, the louder the sound!

But when the Dark Linn
Is aloud from the Rinn
I think of the women the sea-kings brought in:
The women of Dublin, the women who mother
A breed that the land and the sea cannot bother.
In flagons that ream
Like my own river's stream,
That gold of the granite
Gone black in the bogs,
I drink to our Race
That will go to the dogs,
Unless it can trace
And revive the old ways
Of the city when only
The bravest could man it,
Unless it can hold
To the virtues of old
When women resisted
And lovers were bold;
And steer through each upstart
Miasma that clogs
Its mind with the ravings
Of sly pedagogues;
And blow its own trumpet
To shatter the fogs.

TIME, GENTLEMEN, TIME!

O would not Life be charming
  Could we get rid of clocks,
The still ones and alarming
  That break on sleep with shocks,

Then it would be respected
  And worthier far of Man
Than when by springs directed
  From gold or a tin can.

Why should Man's life be reckoned
  By anything so queer
As that which splits the second
  But cannot tell the year?

If we got rid of watches
  The trains would cease to run,
We could not fight a battle-ship
  Or aim a battle gun,

Nor tune the little engines
  Which fill the towns with fumes
And send men with a vengeance
  (Quite rightly) to their tombs.

If we got rid of watches
  And wanted to approach
The pallid peopled cities
  We'd have to hire a coach

And guard, who, to arouse us,
  So hardy in the morn,
Outside the licensed houses
  Would blow a long bright horn.

Our stars know naught of watches,
  There's not a wind that wists
Of mischief that Time hatches
  When handcuffed to our wrists.

No wonder stars are winking,
  No wonder heaven mocks
At men who cease from drinking
  Good booze because of clocks!

'Twould make a devil chortle
  To see how all the clean
Free souls God made immortal
  Must march to a machine.

It makes me wonder whether
  In this grim pantomime
Did fiend or man first blether:
  "Time, Gentlemen, Time!"

We must throw out the timing
  That turns men into gnomes,

Of piece-work and of miming
  That fills the mental homes.

We must get rids of errors,
  And tallies and time checks,
And all the slavish terrors
  That turn men into wrecks.

They have not squared the circle,
  They have not cubed the sphere,
Their calendars all work ill
  Corrected by "leap" year.

But we should all be leaping
  As high as hollyhocks
Did we desist from keeping
  Our trysts with slaves of clocks.

How should we tell the seconds?
  The time a blackbird takes,
To screech across a lane-way,
  And dive into the brakes.

How should we tell the minutes?
  The time it takes to swipe
A lonely pint of Guinness,
  Or load a friendly pipe.

O make the heart Time's measure
  Because, the more it beats,

The more Life fills with pleasure,
  With songs or sturdy feats;

Our clocks our lives are cheating
  They go, and ground we give;
The higher the heart's beating,
  The higher then we live.

AN APPEAL FROM THE JUDGMENT OF PARIS

Stateliness and elegance:
But a kindness in her glance
Gives a lover heart of grace
To appraise her lovely face.
Therefore, though she may not know it,
Sings her humblest, mildest poet
Whom the thought of her makes strong
Thus to challenge with a song,
Challenge Venus' whole entourage
By the virtue of the courage
That her gracefulness engenders,
Grace, the crown of beauty's splendours.

If that young Idalian lout,
When the apple went about
Only had the rare good luck
On her loveliness to look,
What a row there would have been
For, if he had only seen
All the ecstasies and loves
That her limbs make when she moves,
Venus had not had the pippin,
Nor would he have had the strippin'

Of young Leda's swan-white daughter;
Nor had Troy gone down in slaughter.

Paris lived too soon to see
All the sights that ravish me.
I am left alone to grapple
With my love without an apple:
So I sing by her inspired,
Her whose beauty when attired
By good taste can well outdo
All that nude Idalian crew
And still hide sweets; for more, I wis,
The body than the raiment is.

A PRAYER FOR HIS LADY

If it be kindness, God, be kind
To her tall fragrant form and mind
And leave her in this world of ours
Unageing as she is in yours;
And let not Time's contagion blur
The image of your dream in her.

Little enough we have we know
Of Love in Life to lead us through
And Loveliness is on the wing:
Leave the wild cherry with the Spring
In spangling showers to tremble away;
But of your grace preserve the clay.

FOR A BIRTHDAY

When your Birthday comes, I say:
Happy be this holy day!
Happy may it be for you;
But for me it's blessed too
For the fact that I exist
While you live has made it blest.

Had I lived when Helen shone,
All my days would now be gone.
But I live while you are giving
Joy to all who see you living.
Since my happy lot did fall so,
Lady, 'tis my birthday also.

THE ETERNAL RECURRENCE

I thank the gods who gave to me
The yearly privilege to see,
Under the orchards' galaxy,
April reveal her new-drenched skin;
And for the timeless touch within
Whereby I recognise my kin.

TO AN OLD LADY

Where are the eyes that remember your beauty?
Where is the lover whose lingering eyes
Remember the vision by which they were haunted,
Remember the one thing his whole being wanted,
When you took the Spring and his youth by surprise?

Why can we hardly imagine its blooming
When we consider a rose overblown?
Why should the mind with its outlook immortal
Join with those thoughts which dwell more on the portal
Less on the threshold of loveliness gone?

TO A FRIEND IN THE COUNTRY

(Wyckoff, New Jersey)

You like the country better than the town
And very willingly would dwell therein
Afar from the intolerable din
That makes New York a barbarous Babylon;
But far more willingly would I be gone
From all this mad bombardment of the brain
To fields where still and comely thoughts may reign
Deep in your stately mansion old and brown
And colored like a Springtime copper beech:
My God, I would give anything to reach
Your old house standing in the misty rain,
And turn my thoughts to things that do not pass
While gazing through a window at the grass
And wet young oak leaves fingering the pane.

SUNG IN SPRING

The gorse is on the granite,
  The light is growing clear,
Our tilted, tacking planet
  Has another course to steer:
Without a wind to fill her
  She can hold upon the tack.
The Captain's lashed the tiller
  So we dance upon the deck.

Some ships go by a motor,
  And some by sails and spars
But our ship is a rotor
  And she rolls among the stars
And has no fear of crashing:
  Without a spyglass even
You can see the signals flashing
  From the light-houses of Heaven.

Our vessel in her sailing
  Just nods and bowls along,
And half the crew are ailing
  And half are growing strong;
And some make strange grimaces

At us who dance and shout:
The news from outer spaces
    Depends on who looks out.

Some ships by island spices
    Are scented as they run
On through ice precipices
    Behold the midnight sun;
And these go home to haven
    For they are trading ships
But we are touring Heaven
    And we tour in an ellipse.

We do not fear commotions
    Or anything untoward
From rocks or winds or oceans
    We have them all on board
With sea-room all prevailing
    For a never-ending trip;
Was there ever such a sailing?
    Was there ever such a ship?

We have not once been harboured
    Since first we left the slips;
We see to port and starboard
    Brave bright companion ships,
And they go with us roundly;
    But we in hammocks rocked
Shall be sleeping very soundly
    Before our ship is docked.

She leaves no wake behind her,
  No foam before her foot
Because the gods designed her
  A rainbow-rolling boat.
We only know she's rolling
  And all the more we sing
Because just now we're bowling
  And rolling into Spring.

No questions can prevail on
  The Master of the Ship;
He won't say why we sail on
  This never-ending trip:
Though young and old and ailing
  Hold contradictory views
I think that simply sailing
  Is the meaning of the cruise.

ANGELS

In an old court-yard,
Seen from a lane-way,
Down by the Liffey,
Somewhere in Dublin,
Whitened with stone-dust
Dwells an Italian;
And he makes angels.

There are too many
Makers of tomb-stones
Whitened and formally
Carven with crosses,
Dwelling among us:
But he makes angels
Down by the Liffey.

Now I remember
Pagan Pompeii
With its black frescoes
Brightened by Cupids,
Flying attendants,
Winged amorini,
Angels of Venus.

Aye; and I think of
Hermes the Angel,
After his flight from
Crystal Olympus,
Skimming and fanning
With his winged sandals
The violet water;
And in the four-fountained,
Wonderful island,
His thankless reception.

Backwards and forwards
To Middle Ages
Lightly my thought goes
Thinking of Dante
Drawing an angel;
And the tip-pointed
Wings of some airy
Angelic chorus.

What does the poor dusty,
Dublin Italian
Know of the grandeur
Of his great nation?
Grim civilisers,
Law-givers, road-makers,
Founders of cities,
Dreamers of angels,

Far from the sunlight,
Far from the citron,

White, with its branches
Over white tables
Lighted with red wine,
Under grape trellises,
Here in a lane-way,
True to his nature,
Making an angel?

O for ten thousand
Gifted Italians
Dwelling amongst us
Just to put angels
On the black fresco
Of this most dismal,
Reasty and sunless
Town where the meiny
Of Heaven's chief subjects,
The Christ-beloved children,
Are housed in a horrible
Graveyard of houses!

I am a lover
Of Beauty and Splendour,
Lover of Swiftness,
Lover of Brightness,
Lover of sunlight
And the delightful
Movement of water,
Starving in Dublin
For Beauty and Brightness,
Starving for gladness:

God send an angel!
Not a mere figment
From childhood remembered,
God, but a far-flashing
Terrible creature,
An awful tomb-shattering
Burning Idea
Of Beauty and Splendour,
A winged Resurrector,
One with a message
To make the announcement:

Not in His Death,
But in Christ's resurrection
Lieth salvation.

Break down the tenement
Walls that surround them;
Lead out from festering
Lane-way and garden
The Heirs to the Kingdom,
To sunlight, to highland,
To winds blowing over
Green fields; and restore to
The sons of a City,
By seafarers founded,
The sight of white clouds on
An open horizon.

Raise up a man—
What though he must shout from

The mountebank platform
To gain him a hearing—
With knowledge, with vision
And sense of the grandeur
Of human existence,
To plan out a city
As grand, if not grander,
Than Georgian Dublin,
With broadways and side-walks
And dwellings proportioned
To what in the nation
Is faithful and noble;
To save this old town
From the artisan artist,
The cottage replacing
The four-storey mansion,
The cynical largesse
Of hospital-builders;
And all its bad conscience.

Build up with gladness
The house individual
Set in its garden,
Detached and uncrowded;
So that the children
In health grow to greatness;
The family hold to
Its proper distinction;
So that the nation
Be saved from soul-slaughter,
The living damnation,

[36]

Which comes from the crowding
That leads to the Commune.

Build not in lanes
Where the thought of an angel
Is one with a tomb-stone;
But out where Raheny
Gives on to Howth Head
And the winds from Portmarnock;
Or build where Dundrum,
With its foot set in granite,
Begins the long climb
To the hill which O'Donnell
Crossed ages ago
In his flight from the city.
Why should the sons
Of the Gael and the Norseman
Be huddled and cramped
With broad acres about them
And lightning-foot cars
At their beck to transport them,
Which overcome space
Like the sandals of Hermes?

Nations are judged
By their capital cities;
And we by the way
That we fashion an angel.

[37]

ANACHRONISM

Tall and great-bearded: black and white,
The deep-eyed beggar gazed about,
For all his weight of years, upright;
He woke the morning with a shout,
One shout, one note, one rolling word;
But in my dreaming ears I heard
The sea-filled rhythm roll again,
And saw long-vanished boys and men
With eager faces ranged around
A dark man in a market place,
Singing to men of his own race,
With long blithe ripples in the sound,
Of isles enchanted, love and wrath,
And of Achilles' deadly path;
The great ash spear he used to fling;
The bow one man alone could string;
Odysseus in the sea immersed
Who never heard of "Safety First,"
Nor went to a Peace Conference:
For Homer was a man of sense,
And knew right well the only themes
Of Song, when men have time for dreams.
And then, indignant, down the lane
The great dark beggar roared again.

THE ISLES OF GREECE
Applied Poetry
(*Lesbos*)

Marble was her lovely city
And so pleasant was its air
That the Romans had no pity
For a Roman banished there;
Lesbos was a singing island
And a happy home from home
With the pines about its highland
And its crescent faint with form.
Lady, make a nota bene
That Love's lyric fount of glee
Rose in marbled Mytilene
Channelled by the purple sea.
Sappho sang to her hetairai,
And each lovely lyricist
Sappho's singing emulated:
And this point must not be missed
Women were emancipated
Long before the Christian era,
Long before the time of Christ.
Then not only were they equal
To their men folk but themselves;

And the lovely lyric sequel
Lives on all our learned shelves.
Yes; we may be fairly certain,
As results of this release,
Sappho's was, with all its Girton
Girls, the fairest Isle of Greece.

II

Ah, those Isles of Asia Minor!
Was there ever such a coast?
Dawned there any day diviner
On a blither singing host?
Do not give this thought an inning
Lest the critics take it wrong:
In proportion to the sinning
Is the excellence of song.
Sin had not yet been imported
In those days to the Levant,
So the singers loved and sported,
Raised the paean, rhymed the chant,
Until Hebrew fortune tellers
Terrorised the pleasant scene,
Hawking horrors as best-sellers,
Mixing bards and baths with sin.
Therefore pass no moral stricture
On that fairest of Earth's states;
And succumb not to the mixture
Of ideas up with dates.

We shall find as we go boating
(You are paying for the yacht),
That those isles on purple floating
Were the isles of guiltless thought,
Isles whereby a peacock's feather
Would, if cast into the bay,
In the green and purple weather
Be reduced to hodden gray.
Gloomy thoughts are just a failing
From which you must win release
If with me you would come sailing
Carefree through the Isles of Greece.
Therefore pass no surly sentence
From our time and towns fog-pent,
Much less ask for their repentance
Who had nothing to repent.

HIGH ABOVE OHIO

Like a timeless god of old
With one glance I can behold
East and West and men between
On the pleasant, mortal scene.

Looking at them from above
I can see them as they move;
I can tell where they will go;
Where they're coming from I know.

I who with a single glance
See them coming to advance,
Can perceive where they are winning,
See the end in the beginning.

See alternate valleys gleam
Each one with its little stream;
And the undulant, immense,
Free American expanse;

See the rivers on the plain
Break to catch the light again;
And the towns and villages
Islanded by fields and trees.

[42]

And I make a little prayer
As I see the people there,—
For I have not quite forgot
That I share the mortal lot.

God, on Whom Time never bears,
Disregard not mortal years,
For a year to men may be
Precious as eternity.

Look on men in thorpe and town
Walled between the Dawn and Down,
And remember that their cares
Overbalance pleasant years.

Think, when looking through the clouds
At their little streams and woods,
Streams and woods to passing eyes
May present a paradise.

Leave them happy on the earth
Relative to death and birth
Till, in time, their minds transcend
The Beginning and the End.

"AETERNAE LUCIS REDDITOR"

(To Robert Yelverton Tyrrell, Professor of Classics, T. C. D.)

Old Friend, long dead, who yet can thrive
More in my heart than men alive
Because in you the flame lived more
Than ever since the days of yore
When, everywhere that Rome was known,
The post-triumphal silence shone,
And in the vespertinal hush
The trumpet yielded to the thrush:
Because those days you could restore:
Aeternae lucis Redditor.

You shared with us the mood serene
That ruled the universal scene
When Peace was guardian of the poor,
And only rusty was the door
Of Janus, and the pillared shade
Revealed the studious colonnade:
The toga with the purple hem,
The temple that with quiet flame
Acclaimed the distant Emperor,
Aeternae lucis Redditor.

Too seldom on this world of ours
Unwrackt the eternal radiance pours.
Again we shall not see it pour
As in the days and nights before
We lost the wide Virgilian calm;
Days when we sought to earn the palm—
Through the endowment of a wit
Which made us eligible for it—
From you who were Wit's arbiter,
Aeternae lucis Redditor.

'Twixt you and me and me and those
Irremeable the River flows
Since we beheld with joy and awe
The light by which blind Homer saw.
And not again in this our time
Shall sound magnanimous the rhyme;
The wolves have torn our pleasant folds,
And the Great Wall no longer holds.
But Love can bridge the Stygian shore,
Aeternae lucis Redditor.

ELEGY ON THE ARCHPOET
WILLIAM BUTLER YEATS LATELY DEAD

Now that you are a Song
And your life has come to an end
And you wholly belong
To the world of Art, my friend,
Take, for well it is due,
This tribute of my rhymes
With mind unswerved from you
In these enormous times;
Not that I wish to intrude
To mix with mine your leaf,
But that I would entwine
In your magnificent sheaf,
After sad interlude,
A spray cut from that fine
And rare plant, Gratitude.
For anything I owe
In the art of making songs
Largely to you is due,
To you the credit belongs
Who never stinted or spared
Yourself in the difficult feat
Of getting a man prepared
To sing in his own conceit.

None may carry a stone
To your high tower of thought
But surely I can own
Whose was the influence caught
Me in wild wear disguised
And undistinguished found me,
Encouraged, authorized
And with the laurel crowned me,
And make it lovingly clear
While memory is fresh
What manner of man you were
While here clothed on with flesh;
The world knows well your rhymes;
But I would depict you to please
The men in coming times
By a picture of you in these
And make them as grateful to me
As I would be could I find,
Searching past history,
Troubled Euripides,
Or unvexed Sophocles,
By some contemporary mind.

II

The noble head held high,
The nose with an eagle's gaze,
The sharp appraising eye,
The brown unageing face,
The beautiful elegant hands
As white as the breasts of the love

Of Ossian in faerylands:
Among us but ever aloof,
He never hurried or ran,
With eyes on a lordly track,
A tall upstanding man
You dared not slap on the back.
He moved in a diffident way
As if a new-comer to earth
Wrapped in a magical day
Older than death or than birth:
A man come down from the men
Who walked in the morning dew
Of dark Ferdia's strain
With lips like berries of yew:
A race that hosts in the hills,
A race few eyes can see,
A race that our day fills
With perverse, mischievous glee:
A head never turned by fame,
An eerie spirit that takes
Its preternatural calm
From sloe-black mountain lakes.
You heard the sound of his soul
Through words in their equipoise;
The sound of his soul was beautiful:
He had a most beautiful voice.

III

O brain that never lacked full power,
O spirit always in the tower,

That never stooped to earthly lure
But at your height were self-secure:
With wistful child's benignity,
With Man's most noble dignity
You never compromised with fear,
You brought the Brave among us here,
And high above the tinsel scene
Strode with the old heroic mien,
And equalled to your intellect
The grandeur of your self-respect.

IV

O happy were your days on earth
When we sat by the household hearth
And, as the Autumn glow went out,
Bandied the whole bright world about,
Making Reality betray
The edges of sincerer day;
Or in that orchard house of mine,—
The firelight glancing in the wine
Or on your ring that Dulac made—
How merrily your fancy played
With the lost egg that Leda laid,
The lost, third egg Herodotos
In Sparta said he came across;
Or broached a problem more absurd:
In the Beginning was the Word,
Since there was none to hear, unheard?
Or, linking stranger mysteries,
The Spring with dates of the decease

Of Caesar, Christ and Socrates,
You let imagination range
Into the fabulous and strange
Realms of the mind where, at its source,
Life is exultant and perverse.
Then presently you would recite
The verses you made overnight,
Affirming that a song should be
Bone-bare in its simplicity.
Exemplifying this, you chose
Before the Adonais, those
Straight lines of Burns on Matthew Grose:
"For Matthew was a queer man";
Preferring the heartfelt, sincere,
Artless humanity of "queer"
To Shelley's cosmic sermon.
Sometimes you brought invective down
Upon the 'blind and ignorant town'
Which I would half disclaim;
For in my laughing heart I knew
Its scheming and demeaning crew
Was useful as the opposite to
The mood that leads to fame;
For very helpful is the town
Where we by contradicting come
Much nearer to our native home;
But yet it made me grieve
To think its mounted-beggar race
Makes Dublin the most famous place
For famous men to leave:
Where City Fathers staged a farce

And honored one who owned a horse.
They win right well our sneers
Who of their son took no account
Though he had Pegasus to mount
And rode two hemispheres.
Return, Dean Swift, and elevate
Our townsmen to the equine state

V

Now you are gone beyond the glow
As muted as a world of snow;
And I am left amid the scene
Where April comes new-drenched in green,
To watch the budding trees that grow
And cast, where quiet waters flow,
Their hueless patterns below;
And think upon the clear bright rill
That lulled your garden from the hill;
And wonder when shall I be made
Like you, beyond the stream, a shade.

VI

We might as well just save our breath,
There's not a good word to be said for Death
Except for the great change it brings:
For who could bear the loveliest Springs
Touched by the thought that he must keep
A watch eternal without sleep?
But yet within the ends

Of human, not eternal things,
We all resent the change it brings:
Chiefly the loss of friends:
Tyrrell, Mahaffy and Macran,
The last the gentlest gentleman,
And golden Russell—all were gone,
Yet I could turn to you alone.
Now you have turned away
Into the land of sleep or dreams
(If dreams you rule them yet meseems)
With clowns in tragedy.
Here solitary, I, bereft
Of all impulse of praise, am left
Without authority or deft
Example in a rhyme.
I never knew a poet yet
Could put another more in debt.
England's great-hearted Laureate
Is here to testify to that
As, more indebted, I
Whose hand you held, whose line you filled,
Whose mind with reverence instilled
For the most noble and august
Art that can shake men more than lust.
Here I must bide my time
And through my loss grow more content
To go the way the Master went
And follow on a friend
Praising the life by art imbued,
The Apollonian attitude
And lips that murmured metre till the end.

DATE DUE

#47-0108 Peel Off Pressure Sensitive